ESSI
BMX

MW01015596

Written by Simon Mugford
Designed by the Top That! Team

TOP THAT!

Copyright © 2002 Top That! Publishing plc
Tide Mill Way, Woodbridge, Suffolk, IP12 1AP, UK www.topthatpublishing.com
Top That! is a Registered Trademark of Top That! Publishing plc

24 SEVEN Contents

Introduction

BMX (bicycle motocross) biking began in the early 1970s in California, USA. Inspired by the thrills and excitement of motocross, kids began taking their bikes onto tracks, building their own jumps and trying out tricks for themselves. They modified the bikes, but bent wheels and broken frames were a common sight in the streets and parks of the USA. So bicycle manufacturers began to make a new type of bicycle – the BMX.

By 1977, BMX racing was becoming an organised sport. All over the USA, races were being held by individual groups. This led to the formation of the American Bicycle Association (ABA), which continues to organise BMX racing to this day.

By the 1980s, BMX mania had spread all over the world and the BMX was the most popular type of bike, especially among children and teenagers.

BMX bikes need to be tough and resilient. They are built to withstand the shocks caused by jumps and tricks, but at the same time they are lightweight. Some of the best modern BMX bikes are made from aluminium, titanium or even carbon fibre. These machines tend to be expensive, but they are very strong and light.

Handlebars

BMX handlebars are not just to turn the front wheel. They are pushed and pulled in all sorts of directions to lift, twist and turn the bike in the air and on the ground. They are very strong and are made from a tube bent into shape with a cross brace added.

Small Bike

BMX bikes are relatively small – smaller than the average street bike. The standard wheel size is 20 inches, but smaller riders may use 16-inch bikes called minis.

Brakes

Most BMX bikes use standard caliper brakes, where rubber pads grip the wheel. Coaster brakes, which lock the back wheel when pedalling backwards, are used on some freestyle bikes.

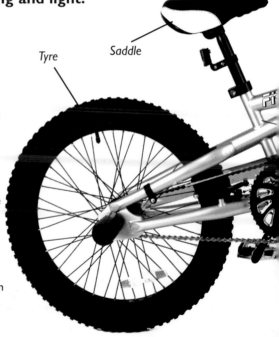

Tyre

Saddle

Frames

The frame is the most important part of the BMX. It is made from three metal tubes welded together to form a triangle. Smaller tubes called stays hold the rear wheel. Most BMX frames are made from a special steel called chrome-moly.

Tricking Out

Many BMX riders buy parts for their bikes to make them stronger or lighter. Adding these 'aftermarket' parts is known as 'tricking out' a bike.

No Gears

Unlike mountain bikes, BMX bikes have no gears – just a fixed chain and sprocket. The size of the sprocket depends on the BMX style the bike is designed for.

Spokes or Mags?

Racing BMX bikes usually have lightweight aluminium- or steel-spoked wheels. For extra strength, freestyle bikes may have mag wheels made from a tough, moulded plastic.

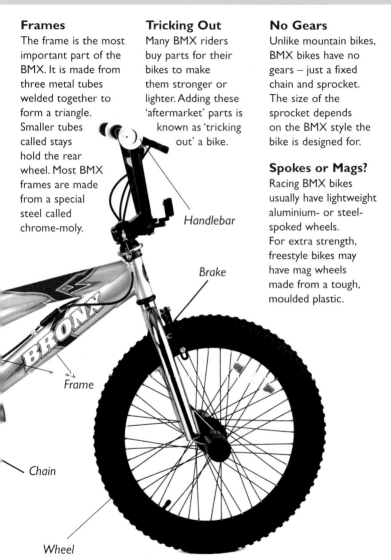

Handlebar

Brake

Frame

Chain

Wheel

BMX racing bikes are generally lighter than those used for freestyle – less weight means more speed! The race bike is a pretty basic machine, designed purely for speed on a dirt track. Many professional racers will build bikes to their own specification, stripping them down and customising them for their own needs.

Chain

When you pedal it is the chain that will turn the back wheel. Chains come in different thicknesses, 410 is best for racing.

Saddle

Brake

Tyres

The tyres used in BMX racing are designed to give good grip on a dirt track. Wide and with a deep tread, they are known as knobbies. Some racers change the tyre pressure according to the surface, making them softer on a hard track.

Tyre

Frame

Racing bikes tend to be larger than other BMX types and so the frame will be longer. The extra length helps to provide stability. Racing frames are often made of aluminium.

Wheels

Most racing bikes have 20-inch spoked wheels. Bikes with 26-inch wheels, called cruisers, are sometimes used by older riders for racing. These race in a separate class.

Frame

Handlebar

Chain

Brakes

Some BMX racing bikes only have a rear brake. This reduces weight and helps prevent accidents – a sudden stop with a front brake can send the rider over the handlebars.

Wheel

Freestyle **BMX** bikes evolved from the original racing bikes. They have much heavier frames than racing bikes and are designed to withstand the impact caused by jumps and tricks. Some freestyle bikes have 'oversize' frames – extra large tubes designed for even more strength. They are also fitted with accessories and features that allow the rider to perform tricks.

Smooth Tyres

Most freestyle bikes have smooth tyres fitted, rather than the deep-tread knobbies used in racing. These provide better grip and manoeuvrability on concrete, tarmac and wooden ramps.

Dirt Jumpers

Bikes designed for dirt jumping have the heavy frame and strong wheels used in freestyle, but have longer top tubes. This helps the rider perform tricks while in the air. Dirt jumpers usually have one brake, like a racing BMX.

Saddle

Tyre

Brake

Flatland Bikes

BMX bikes used for flatland freestyle riding are much more compact than other types of BMX. They have a shorter frame, smaller handlebars and a smaller chain sprocket.

High Pressure

Flatland involves a lot of impact between the tyres and the ground, so the tyres are designed for higher pressures.

Rotors

Some freestyle tricks involve turning the handlebars through 360°. The bikes are fitted with rotors, which allow this to be done without the brake cables becoming tangled.

Pegs

Foot pegs of different sizes can be fitted to the front and rear wheel axles. These help the rider perform certain tricks and stunts.

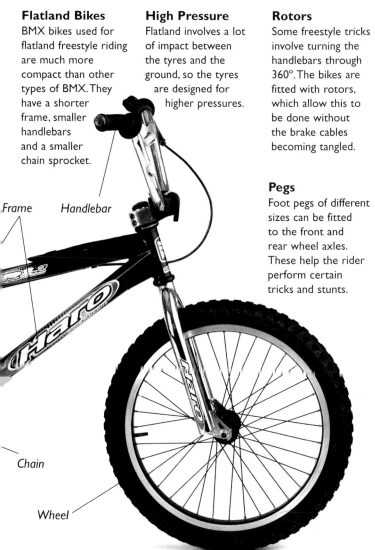

Frame

Handlebar

Chain

Wheel

BMX riding has divided into a number of different styles. The 'street' culture where BMX began is probably best shown in the flatland and park styles, where riders perform many types of wild tricks. Though they share a similar background, they are pretty different and many fans are fiercely loyal to one or the other.

Park or Street?

Park riding used to be known as street riding, because it began in the streets. As skateparks have become more common and the style has featured in competitions, it has become known as park.

Jump 'n' Grind

Park riders ride their bikes over ramps and jumps and grind them along walls and other obstacles.

Public Parks

In some towns and cities, there are public skateparks where BMX riders and skateboarders meet up and practise their tricks. The rivalry between riders and skaters is a friendly one and some of the BMX tricks have been adapted from skate tricks.

Which Surface?

Most of the outdoor skateparks are made from concrete, though there are some made from wood. Most wooden parks are indoors and provide a softer landing than concrete. Some parks are made from metal, though these are not popular with riders.

Flatland

Flatland, as its name suggests, is done on a flat surface. The key to flatland riding is balance and flexibility. Riders get into outrageous positions, balancing their bikes, hopping around and throwing them from one position to another.

Popularity

Flatland riding has gained popularity over recent years. It can be practised in pretty much any open space – you don't need any ramps or jumps. Flatlanders often become devoted to the experience, spending hour after hour practising their moves. They enjoy themselves so much they don't mind getting hurt a little.

Originality

Flatland is often considered to be the most original and creative of all the BMX styles. New tricks are being invented all the time and flatland riders have a reputation for being a bit weird!

BMX Racing

Modern **BMX** racing is a highly organised sport. Races are held at regional and national levels and riders start as young as six. Many keep racing until they are well into their twenties! **BMX** racing is a great way of meeting new friends and it's also good exercise. Parents get involved too, helping out around the track and showing their support.

Dirt Tracks

BMX races take place on dirt tracks, either outdoors or in a large arena. The race starts on a small hill, where the racers line up behind a gate. The key to being a successful racer is to execute a good start and to negotiate the jumps at the fastest speed possible. You should try to start with both feet on the pedals and keep low for the jumps.

The start of a race.

Turns

BMX tracks feature left, right, flat and banked turns. Banked turns, or berms, are good places to overtake other riders.

Whoops!

Parts of the track will feature lots of small bumps that shake the bike and the rider. These are called whoop-de-doos, or whoops.

Jumps

The big jumps with long, flat tops – the ones that send riders flying – are called tabletops. Double or triple jumps are big jumps that are close together.

Dirt jumping is a style of BMX that combines the jumps and tricks of freestyle with the off-road thrills of mountain biking. In fact, many dirt jumpers use ATB (mountain) bikes for this style. In some ways, dirt jumping goes back to the original DIY attitude of BMX, with riders building their own jumps and trails.

Beginnings

Dirt jumping began in places where there was nowhere for freestyle fans to do their jumps and tricks. It was also inspired by the craze for mountain biking, which began in the late 1980s.

Trails

Dirt jumpers build trails anywhere there is a good deal of dirt! Areas of wasteland and woodland are popular hangouts for dirt jumping fans. You must always ask for permission from the owner of the land before building a trail.

Building Jumps

Building jumps is hard work. You and your friends will need some shovels to pile up the dirt. Pack the dirt down and then moisten it with water (or hope it rains). When the jump dries hard, you're ready to go!

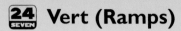

Riding ramps, better known as vert (as in vertical), is the most extreme part of park or street riding.

Halfpipe

The full-sized, vertical halfpipe is the most challenging of all ramps. Riders can ride the halfpipe from end to end without losing any momentum.

The part where the ramp curves is called the 'transition' – the vert is the amount of vertical surface after the transition.

The centre of the ramp is known as the flat and the 'shelf' at the top, where riders watch others perform, is called a deck. Big transitions and verts allow the most spectacular tricks.

Getting big air on a halfpipe

Big air

Performing aerial tricks and turns on a halfpipe is what all park BMXers aspire to – they want to get some 'big air'. Most skateparks will feature smaller halfpipes – midi or mini ramps – for people to practise on.

Quarterpipe

The quarterpipe is an essential part of any good skatepark. They are used for aerial tricks in the same way as halfpipes, but they also allow riders to redirect themselves and pick up speed for other ramps around the park.

A single quarterpipe

BMX riding is now a professional sport. Yes, there are some very lucky, talented young people who make money riding ramps and thrashing around on their bikes. They take part in competitions all over the world. The best-known event is the Summer X Games, which since 1995 has featured the best in BMX freestyle along with skateboarding, in-line skating and other extreme sports.

All Disciplines

Competitions feature all three freestyle disciplines – park, vert and flatland. Competitors can enter into any of the events, although most specialise in one or two. It's common to compete in both park and vert.

Team Riding

Freestylers can compete alone or as

opposite directions and crossing each other in the air.

Judging

The judging in freestyle competition is similar to that used in ice skating and gymnastics. A panel of experts award points for control, style and originality.

part of a team. The doubles vert is a popular team event, with pairs of riders riding ramps in

Routines

There are certain moves that the competitors are required to do. They then perform an original routine. A smoothly performed, highly original routine will earn a lot of points.

Music

Many of the routines are performed to music. Competitors can choose the music they wish to perform to – they will try to pick something suited to their routine. This adds to the atmosphere and excitement of the event.

Sponsorship

Big competitions attract sponsorship from large companies. National teams are sponsored, usually by bike or equipment manufacturers.

Growth

Big competitions also help to generate interest in the sport. Professional riders spend huge amounts of time practising on better and better bikes. This means that the tricks are getting ever more spectacular.

The Summer X Games

Now attended by over 250,000 spectators, the Summer X Games attract over 400 athletes, all determined to show their talent for gravity-defying sports.

Action from the Summer X Games

Most people get a BMX because they want to do some tricks. Sure, they will use them to get to school or see their friends, but thrashing around pulling wheelies, endos and bunny hops is what it's really all about. Doing BMX tricks takes some practice and you need to start by mastering the basics.

Know Your Bike

Before you start doing tricks, get to know your bike. Find out how responsive it is to turns and braking. When you feel sure that you can control your BMX comfortably, you can start doing tricks.

Wheelies

The wheelie is one of the first tricks that BMX riders learn to do. Whilst pedalling, you pull up the handlebars and lift the front wheel in the air. You keep moving on just the back wheel, using your weight to balance yourself and the bike.

Manual

A manual is a simple variation of the wheelie. On a quarterpipe or halfpipe the rider does a wheelie across the top deck before returning to the ramp.

Wheelie

Speed Jumps

Knowing how to take jumps at speed is essential for BMX racers. You need to pull a small wheelie just as the front wheel hits the top of the bump. Sitting back over the rear wheel will keep it on the ground as it goes over the bump.

Skidding

If you are racing over dirt tracks or riding trails, you'll need to get used to skidding. Practising skids and learning how to control them will help you to go faster around turns. Practise on dirt or grass to prevent wearing your tyres out quickly.

Taking Corners

You need to lean with your bike to take corners at speed. This helps to control skids, keeps you balanced on the bike and gets you round the corner faster.

Skidding

Endos

In an endo, the back wheel is lifted into the air. Pedal slowly in a straight line, lean forward and pull hard on the front brake. Don't go too fast or lean too far forward – you'll go over the handlebars!

Curb Endos

You can also do an endo against a curb. Pedal slowly up to a curb. When the front wheel hits the curb, push forward on the handlebars and jump up to bring the rear wheel up. Always keep your pedals level when doing endos.

A curb endo

Basic Skills and Tricks

(1)

(2)

(3)

Bunny Hops
The bunny hop is a basic flatland jump. Pedal up to a speed where the bike will freewheel for about five seconds. With the pedals level, lean forward and pull the bike up at the same time.

Jumping Boxes
It's a good idea to practise bunny hops over objects – that way you can tell how you're getting on. Shoeboxes are ideal

Bunny hop

for practising bunny hops because they just collapse if you land on them.

Getting Higher
When you feel confident doing bunny hops, you could try doing them onto curbs. The more you practise, the higher and longer you'll be able to jump.

(4)

Once you've learned how to control your bike and mastered the basic skills and tricks, you can start trying some complicated stuff. There are lots of different names and variations of tricks, because riders give new names to tricks as they add their own little 'twists' or variations. These 'advanced' tricks often feature in freestyle competitions.

Can-Can

This is when a rider takes a foot off a pedal and stretches one leg over the frame so that both legs are on the same side of the bike.

Cross-Up (X-up)

A cross-up involves twisting the bike whilst in the air. After coming off a ramp or a bump, turn the handlebars to the left or right. Turn them back straight again before landing.

Cross-up

Kickout

The kickout is another trick done in the air. It's a bit like a cross-up in reverse. As the bike leaves the ground, twist your hips to one side. This makes the rear of the bike swing out with the front wheel pointing forward.

Kickout

Tabletop

The tabletop is a kickout taken a step further. You need to kick the bike out so it's positioned horizontally in the air. If you ride with your left foot forward, tabletop to the right. Tabletop to the left if you like your right foot forward. The tabletop is a strangely addictive trick. No matter how many times you attempt it you'll come back for more, determined to perfect the move.

Tabletop

Kickturn

The kickturn is a park trick done on a ramp or quarterpipe. The idea is to turn the bike around 180° (half a circle) on the back wheel. Halfway up the ramp, lift the front wheel as high as you can and lean to the left or right. When you are facing the way you came, bring the front wheel back down and pedal away in that direction.

Kickturn

Aerial 180°

This trick is a bit like a kickturn done in the air. When the bike takes off at the end of a quarterpipe, you need to use your weight to swing the bike right around. The rear wheel must come down on the ramp first.

Aerial 180°

360°

The 360° aerial is the natural next step from the 180°. To do this trick, you need to turn the bars as in the cross-up, then swing your hips to bring the bike right around to the way it was. This trick takes a lot of practice.

No footer

No Footer

In this trick, you take your feet off the pedals for as long as possible while the bike is in the air. Sounds easy, but you need to practise on the ground first. If the bike

lands with your feet off the pedals, don't try to put them back on – you'll get hurt.

Bar Hop

To do this flatland trick, get the bike going

forward at a medium speed. Sitting down, lift your knees up to your chin and straighten your legs out over the handlebars. Front pegs are useful to rest your feet on.

29

Becoming a pro **BMX** rider takes years of practice – the top professionals are all in their twenties. Spectacular aerial tricks are favourites with the pro riders in vert competitions and are generally the most exciting for the spectators. However, the tricky balancing acts of the flatlanders are equally exciting and take some time to master.

Tailwhip

In a tailwhip, you stand on the front wheel as the bike swings round. This is a bit like a simple endo taken to extremes! The rider pulls an endo, stands on the front wheel, swings the bike right around and rides off.

Superman

The superman is one of the most popular aerial tricks among pro riders and spectators alike. It requires a jump that gives a lot of height and you need to get up a lot of speed. The superman is basically a no footer taken to the next level. When the rider takes his feet off the pedals, he starts to kick them backwards. He must keep the bike as level as possible. At the height of the jump, he extends his arms and legs out as far as he can, pushing the bike away from him. He can't let the bike tilt to either side, otherwise he'll wipe out. To get back on the bike, he pulls it in with his arms and then jumps back on the pedals. Keeping the bike as level as possible, he brings it back to the ground and rides away.

Superman

Backflip

In a backflip, rider and bike do a complete somersault before coming back down on the ramp. You need a lot of air and a lot of strength to pull this trick off. Needless to say, it's extremely dangerous and really only for the pros.

Corkscrew

The corkscrew is based on the snowboarding trick of the same name. It is very exciting to watch, but extremely difficult to do. A favourite trick of professional freestyler Dave Mirra, the corkscrew refers to any very fast and tight rotation performed off-axis.

Barspin

The barspin involves spinning the bars right round when the bike is in the air. The rider has to grip the seat with his thigh and then spin the bars as quickly as possible. It's important to grab the bars before the bike lands!

Barspin

BMX biking, like any other sport, has its milestones, records and people who have really made an impact. Here are a few 'fast facts' about the wild world of BMX riding.

Pedal Cross

With its roots in motocross riding, BMX was called 'pedal cross' by some early riders. Fortunately the name didn't stick – BMX sounds much better, doesn't it?

Big Hop

The world record for a bunny hop was set in 1983 by American rider Dave Sanderson. He hopped his bike to a height of 1.01m (42 inches).

Big Air

The greatest height reached off a BMX jump is 8.08 m (26.5 ft). It was achieved by Matt Hoffman in 2001 on a 24-foot high quarterpipe.

Power Jump

Pro rider Colin Winkelmann achieved a ramp jump of 35.63 m (116 ft 11 in) at Agoura Hills, California on 20 December 2000. His BMX was towed behind a motorcycle at a speed approaching 100 km/h (60 mph).

Dave Mirra in action

Double Backflip

Dave Mirra achieved the first double backflip in a BMX competition.

Redline

Redline Bicycles built the first BMX. Its founder, Linn Kastan, manufactured motorcycle frames, and saw the potential for the growing BMX craze.

Backflip

The backflip was first achieved and perfected by José Yanez.

Trickster

Jay Miron is one of the most prolific trick inventors in the world of BMX. He was the first rider to perfect double barspins, 540° tailwhips and double backflips.

BMX Star

Hollywood actress Nicole Kidman starred in the 1983 BMX movie, *BMX Bandits*, a mad-cap crime caper. She played BMX-riding teenager Judy. An unknown teenager at the time, she went on to become a Hollywood superstar, appearing in films such as *Far and Away*, *To Die For*, *Moulin Rouge* and *The Others*.

Nicole Kidman (right) in BMX Bandits

Freestyle Firsts

The first organised freestyle contests took place in the early 1980s in concrete skateparks on the West Coast of the USA.

AFA

In 1984, the American Freestyle Association (AFA) was formed and it held two major flatland and ramp events in California.

Matt Hoffman

After a decline in the late 1980s, Matt Hoffman revitalised BMX with the Bicycle Stunt (BS) Series, which began in 1992. It included vert, park and flatland categories and triggered the modern BMX craze.

Dave Mirra

Dave Mirra is one of the world's top BMX riders. He is the most successful BMX competitor at the X Games, picking up twelve medals for street and vert in his years of competition.

Matt Hoffman

Getting started in BMX isn't difficult, but there are a few things you should consider before you get going. Do you want to race, ride ramps or go dirt jumping? If you want to race, will your parents help you get to the events? If you want to be a freestyler, are you prepared to practise, practise, practise?

Where?

If you're into freestyle, you'll need somewhere to practise those tricks. Flatlanders can do their stuff in empty car parks or any quiet street. Park and vert riders will need access to a decent skatepark.

Buying a Bike

A major consideration for buying a BMX (or any bike) is cost. You don't need a really expensive bike to start racing or freestyling, but a cheap bike won't last long. It's better to buy a decent bike that will last.

Ask Around

You'll probably be interested in getting into BMX if your mates are. Ask them for some advice, look out for magazines and check the 'Find Out More' page at the back of this book.

Maintenance

The bike needs to be stripped down regularly. The chainguard, reflectors and any axle pegs will need to be removed. Your bike should be properly maintained, whichever style you are into. A poorly maintained bike will not only not win any races, it could be dangerous, too.

Tool Kit

You will need a few tools such as tyre levers, crank remover, chain tool and various-sized wrenchs and sockets.

Wheels

Make sure the spokes are tight and that none are broken. There should be no dents or buckles in the rims and the wheel should not be loose on its bearings.

Tyres

Make sure that your tyres are always in good condition. No matter what style of BMX you do, they're going to take a pounding.

Chain

Make sure the chain has the right amount of tension. It is important that it is also kept oiled regularly.

Brakes

Very important. Make sure the cables are not frayed or kinked and that the calipers are adjusted and working properly.

BMX riding is a thrilling sport in all its various styles. The potential for injury is obvious to any spectator – falling from a big air jump or colliding with another racer can be very painful. Crashing and falling is part of what BMX riding is all about, but serious riders take steps to reduce the risk of injury.

Bike Pads

Falling onto the top tube or the handlebar can be very painful. For this reason, many riders will pad out their bikes to protect themselves.

Shoes

Comfortable training shoes are best for footwear when BMX riding. Make sure they are hard-wearing enough to protect your feet.

Clothes

Long-sleeved shirts and trousers protect against grazes. Some clothes come with padding built into the hips, knees and elbows. Elbow pads are compulsory in many competitions.

Helmets

It may not look cool at the local skatepark, but the helmet is the most important piece of BMX protective gear. Racers tend to wear full-face helmets while freestylers wear open-face types with a separate mouthguard. Wearing a helmet is compulsory in competition.

The world of **BMX** is full of strange-sounding names for tricks and bike parts. The language developed along with the street culture where **BMX** began. Many of the terms come from skateboarding and other extreme sports. This glossary contains some of the words found in this book and others that you may hear at your local skatepark or race track.

Aftermarket A component or product that's not part of the original bike.

Amped Stoked, thrilled, pumped up.

Apex The sharpest point in a corner.

ATB All Terrain Bike; i.e. mountain bike, or MTB.

Bail To ditch your bike before a crash.

Bank Any sloped area under 90°.

Barspin Spinning the handlebars a full rotation or more and grabbing them again before landing.

Berm The sloped bank of a turn.

Berm warfare Using the berm tactically to beat opponents.

Box jump Jump used in street competitions. It's made from two ramps on either side of a 10-foot high deck.

Brain bucket A helmet.

Can-Can When a rider takes one foot off a pedal and stretches their leg over the frame so that both legs are on the same side of the bike.

Canyon The sunken area between ramps in dirt and the empty space between two ramps in street.

Chunder To crash.

Corndog When a rider is covered in dust, often after falling.

Cross-up In the air, turning the handlebars as far as they will go in one direction without releasing the grip, then turning them back in the other direction before landing. Also known as an x-up.

Dab When a rider puts their foot down and touches the ground in order to maintain balance.

Double A series of two jumps placed close enough together to enable a rider to make both with one jump.

Double Can-Can When the rider moves one leg to the other side of the bike, then brings the other leg up to meet it.

Endo Bringing the rear of the bike into the air whilst stopped on the front wheel.

Fun box A four-sided box jump (ramp on every side) found in street courses.

Freestyle Any type of BMX trick riding.

Grind To ride on an object like a ledge or handrail with anything but the wheels making contact.

Halfpipe A type of ramp that is shaped like a 'U' and used for vert riding.

Hammer To ride as hard as possible.

Kicker A name for a jump ramp. Kickers are used for height rather than distance.

Knee pad Protective padding worn on the knees.

Knee slide A way of controlling a fall by sliding on plastic caps on the knee pads.

Knobbies Tyres with thick treads. Usually used in racing.

Lid A helmet.

Lip The top edge of the halfpipe.

Lip trick Any trick performed on or near the lip of the halfpipe.

Mad Crazy, or 'a lot'.

Manual Where a rider does a wheelie across the top deck before returning to the ramp.

No hander lander Landing a jump with no hands on the bars.

No footer/no hander Taking feet/hands off the bike while in the air.

Nose wheelie Where a rider rides the front wheel while the back wheel is in the air.

Nothing When a rider fully lets go of his bike with his hands and feet in the air so that no part of his body is touching the bike.

Obstacles Jumps, handrails – anything a rider uses to do tricks.

Off axis When a rider is tilted slightly to the left or right.

One footer/one hander Any air pulled with one foot/hand off the bike.

Park Term for street riding.

Phat Cool or 'a lot'.

Poser Someone who acts better than they are.

Quarterpipe A halfpipe with one wall.

Run A series of tricks in a sequence.

Scuffing Using the feet on the tyres for tricks.

Seat post Post to which the seat is attached.

Seat tube Vertical bicycle frame tube. The tube into which the seat post is inserted.

Semi-slicks Tyres with low-profile tread.

Sick Big, crazy, cool – incredibly difficult.

Skid lid A helmet.

Slicks Tyres with no tread.

Spine ramp Two halfpipes placed back to back to create a double 'U' shape.

Squirrelly Slightly out of control.

Stall When a rider pauses briefly before dropping back into the ramp.

Superman Where a rider takes both feet off the pedals in the air and stretches his legs as far behind the bike as possible.

Tabletop When a rider flattens his bike out into the horizontal plane in the air, then straightens it back out to land. Also a flat-topped jump used in races.

Tailwhip Where a rider whips his bike around the axis of the handlebars, whilst keeping the handlebars and his body stationary and lands back on the bike before hitting the ground.

Taking air Jumping on a bike with both wheels leaving the ground.

Thrashing Riding BMX and doing tricks for fun.

Tombstone A vertical portion of a ramp that rises above the top of the ramp to add more vert.

Transition The point where a ramp or jump goes from the horizontal plane to the vertical plane.

Tricking out Adding parts to, or modifying, a bike for racing.

Turndown Where a rider turns the handlebars and his body down towards the ground while the rest of the bike stays facing straight up.

Vert Riding the halfpipe.

Wall Any bank that is at or above 90°.

Wallride To ride on a wall that has no transition.

Wash out When the front tyre loses traction, especially when going around a corner.

Wild pigs Squeaky brakes.

Wipeout A crash.

Wonky When things aren't functioning properly.

X-Up See cross-up.

Zonk Hit the wall…

If you want to find out more about **BMX**, there are plenty of magazines and places on the Net that can answer your questions. Check out magazines or visit the websites below.

British Cycling Federation

This organisation represents all kinds of cycling in the United Kingdom.
Their website is:
www.bcf.uk.com

BMX Canada

To find out about BMX in Canada visit:
www.chasebmxmag.com

American Bicycle Association

The ABA is the world's largest BMX sanctioned organisation. To find out more, go to:
www.ababmx.com

BMX New Zealand

For BMX in New Zealand go to:
www.bmxnz.gq.nu

BMX Australia

Find out about all things BMX and Australian at:
www.bmxaustralia.com.au

Practise Those Tricks

Get tips on the tricks at:
www.bmxtrix.com

BMX Online

The BMX Online magazine is a good place to check out all the latest BMX news:
www.bmxonline.com

EXPN

Find out about BMX and all things extreme at X Games organisers EXPN:
www.expn.go.com